BUILD STRONG COMMUNITIES

BY MARIBEL VALDEZ GONZALEZ

CAPSTONE PRESS
a capstone imprint

Published by Capstone Press, an imprint of Capstone
1710 Roe Crest Drive, North Mankato, Minnesota 56003
capstonepub.com

Library of Congress Cataloging-in-Publication Data
Names: Gonzalez, Maribel Valdez, author.
Title: Build strong communities / by Maribel Valdez Gonzalez.
Description: North Mankato, Minnesota : Capstone Press, [2022] | Series: Social justice and you | Includes bibliographical references and index. | Audience: Ages 8–11 | Audience: Grades 4–6 | Summary: "It's not always easy to understand the experiences of people who are different from us. But we have to work at it to build better communities. In this book, you'll learn about practicing empathy, communicating respectfully, and building meaningful community with other people. With kid-friendly explanations of key ideas and relevant scenarios, this text will help young kids be engaged, respectful members of their community"—Provided by publisher.
Identifiers: LCCN 2022008471 (print) | LCCN 2022008472 (ebook) |
ISBN 9781666345414 (hardcover) | ISBN 9781666345438 (paperback) |
ISBN 9781666345445 (pdf) | ISBN 9781666345469 (kindle edition)
Subjects: LCSH: Communities—Juvenile literature. | Community development—Juvenile literature. | Minorities—Juvenile literature. | Gender identity—Juvenile literature.
Classification: LCC HM756 .G65 2022 (print) | LCC HM756 (ebook) | DDC 307—dc23/eng/20220330
LC record available at https://lccn.loc.gov/2022008471
LC ebook record available at https://lccn.loc.gov/2022008472

Editorial Credits
Editor: Ericka Smith; Designer: Sarah Bennett; Media Researcher: Julie De Adder;
Production Specialist: Katy LaVigne

Image Credits
Getty Images: coja1108, 17, energy, 15, Gary John Norman, 18 (top), insta_photos, 7, kali9, 22, monkeybusinessimages, 5, Richard Hutchings, 23, Zave Smith, 14; Shutterstock: A Sharma, 11, Cienpies Design, cover, Erin Alexis Randolph, 8, Jacek Chabraszewski, 27, Johnny Silvercloud, 12, Joke_Phatrapong, 28, Liderina, 25, Lopolo, 29, Magnia (background), back cover and throughout, Monkey Business Images, 20, Suzette Leg Anthony, 21, tawanroong, 18 (bottom)

All internet sites appearing in back matter were available and accurate when this book was sent to press.

TABLE OF CONTENTS

Words in **bold** are in the glossary.

YOU AND YOUR COMMUNITY

We all belong to different communities. Our schools are communities. Our towns are communities. All we want is to be our authentic—or true—selves in those communities. For our communities to be safe for everyone, we must know ourselves. And we must learn about others. That way we can understand everyone's experiences. And we can treat one another with respect.

Maybe **Latine** students at your school have a different experience than students who don't hold that identity. And Latine students who are **queer** will have different experiences from those who are not. What might a school that respects all those experiences look like?

GROUP IDENTITIES AND INTERSECTIONALITY

Our group or social identities are how we are grouped with other people. They include our race, ethnicity, gender, sexual identity, abilities, religion, and class status. In every community, people who hold different identities have different experiences.

When our experiences are different because of multiple identities that we hold, it's called intersectionality. It helps explain why a Black girl's experience will be different from a white girl's experience and a Black boy's experience.

CHAPTER 1

YOU DON'T HAVE TO BE LIKE ME

In an **inclusive** community, it's okay to be different. People can connect around what they have in common. Everyone needs to feel accepted. But some communities may not feel inclusive for all people.

In the United States, people who are not white, **heterosexual**, or **cisgender** are often excluded because they are different. A gay student might be teased by his classmates. Latine people may not often see themselves in movies. A company may not consider the needs of **transgender** employees before making a dress code policy.

A community may not feel inclusive because of its history. Some groups may have been excluded or harmed in the past. Those actions may still continue. Or the effects of those actions might still influence how people treat one another.

PRIVILEGE

If someone has privilege, they experience advantages just because they're a member of a certain group. In the U.S., someone might experience privilege because they are heterosexual, cisgender, or white. For example, white people can read books or watch movies and expect to read about or see people who look and act like them. People of color don't usually have the same expectations.

In the U.S., for example, **colonizers** used violence and cheating to take land from **Indigenous** nations. Survivors were often pushed onto **reservations**. The government didn't honor agreements with Indigenous nations. And it kept many Indigenous people from practicing their traditions.

These actions isolated Indigenous people. They also affected Indigenous nations' ability to support themselves. So Indigenous people on reservations often experience poverty. Indigenous cultures are often less visible and less respected in the U.S. too.

People protesting an oil pipeline that would run through an Indigenous nation's land

Knowing history helps us think about how best to interact with one another. It's important to understand why people have certain experiences. It's also important to not continue excluding and harming people who are different from us.

IDEAS IN ACTION

During morning circle, Ms. Del Rosario said to her fifth graders, "Good morning! Will each person share their favorite meal and why it's their favorite?"

Alyssa went first. "My favorite meal is the fry bread Shimá makes. We eat it with soups and chili. We also make tacos with it."

Alec raised his hand. Ms. Del Rosario asked, "Alec, do you have a wondering or a compliment for Alyssa?"

Alec replied, "I have a wondering. What does *Shimá* mean?"

Alyssa was happy to answer. "It is a Navajo or Diné word for my mom. You say *Shimá* with an emphasis on the *a*," she explained.

Ms. Del Rosario replied, "Thank you for teaching us! Let's all practice saying it together."

The entire class slowly and loudly repeated, "Shimaaaa."

Which part of her identity did Alyssa share?

How did the class celebrate cultural differences?

CHAPTER 2

USING EMPATHY

We all experience emotions like happiness, sadness, and fear. Empathy is the ability to understand and share the feelings of others. Empathy helps us understand people who are different from us. We may not understand what the other person is going through, but we can share their emotions.

Empathy is an important part of good relationships. It decreases misunderstandings and disagreements, and it leads to kindness. And it leads to helpful behaviors.

Many people are excluded or harmed because of their identity. They might experience racism, transphobia—unfair treatment of transgender people—or **ableism**. It's important that people who haven't experienced a particular form of **oppression** try to understand the perspective of those who have.

When people who are oppressed speak up about their experiences, we should practice empathy. They might feel angry, afraid, or even lonely. Practicing empathy helps us show care about what they're going through. It helps us show them that they matter and that we want them to live freely. And it helps build strong communities.

IDEAS IN ACTION

During recess, Vanessa walked away from her friend Sarah and over to the slide by herself. She started to cry as she slid down.

Jim saw her crying. "Are you okay?" he asked.

Vanessa replied, "Sarah said that my dark skin makes me look ugly."

Jim felt sad too. He replied, "I am sorry. That must make you feel sad. Your skin isn't ugly."

Vanessa smiled a little when he said that, and they began to chat.

Why was Vanessa sad?

How did Jim show her empathy?

Have you ever felt sad for a friend? What did you do?

We practice empathy best when everyone feels safe enough to share. We can help create this safe, trusting feeling by being willing to share things about ourselves.

We can also create trust by admitting when we've hurt someone. When we're learning from one another, we will make mistakes. But we must be willing to own the impact of our actions, even if we didn't mean to hurt someone. An example of owning the impact of our actions is saying, "I am sorry that I hurt you."

CHAPTER 3

GETTING THE LANGUAGE RIGHT

Just like getting someone's name right, using the right language to talk about someone's identities is important. It's a way to show respect to others. The words we use to describe identities often change, though. So you'll probably make a mistake. That's okay! You can make it right.

GENDER

Gender is about how a person feels inside. People can hold many different gender identities. They might identify as a boy. They might identify as a girl. Or they might not identify as a boy or as a girl. They might instead identify as **nonbinary**. These are just a few ways someone might identify. And how someone feels might change too.

Sometimes our clothes and our hairstyles help show our gender identity. Sometimes they don't. Don't assume a person's gender identity based on how they look.

You can show respect for different gender identities by sharing your pronouns and using other people's pronouns. These are some common pronouns:

- she/her
- he/him
- they/them

Ask people their pronouns. If you accidentally use the wrong pronouns, correct yourself. Then keep practicing. You can also start conversations by sharing your pronouns.

IDEAS IN ACTION

Mark was excited to go back to school after the holiday break in December. When he went to his classroom, there was a new student sitting at the desk next to him. Mark could tell that they looked a little nervous.

"Hi! I'm Mark. I use the pronouns *he* and *him*," he said.

"Hi, Mark. I'm Noah. My pronouns are *they* and *them*," Noah replied. They looked a little less nervous.

"You're new, right? Do you want to play together at recess?" Mark asked.

How did Mark show acceptance of different gender identities?

How did Noah respond?

RACE AND ETHNICITY

When talking about people's racial and ethnic identities, it is important not to guess. Asking people how they identify is a way to honor who they are.

In the U.S., people often use four racial categories—Indigenous, Black, Asian, and white. And there are a lot of ethnic identities. People may identify many ways based on their preferences about their racial and ethnic identities.

Some people identify as African American, while others identify as Black. Some people identify as Indigenous. Others might use Native American. Or they identify with their Indigenous nation, such as Mohawk or Jamestown S'Klallam.

Latine is a word some use to describe people whose culture is from Latin American countries. But not everyone identifies this way. People might use other words, like *Hispanic* or *Chicane*.

DISABILITY

There are different ways to describe a person with a disability. People with disabilities make their own choices about language. Always ask the person what they prefer.

Some people prefer person-first, while others prefer identity-first language. Person-first language puts a focus on the person before their disability. Someone might describe themselves as a "person with autism." Identity-first language centers their disability more. A person who prefers that language might describe themselves as an "autistic person."

CHAPTER 4

BUILDING CONNECTIONS

How have you made friends at school or in your neighborhood? How did you get to know each other? When you care about someone, you're curious about them. Friends ask each other questions. They learn about each other's interests.

You can build connections with people who are different from you by practicing the same things. You should try to understand them and their culture. Here are some questions you can ask:

- What are your pronouns?
- What is your favorite holiday? How do you celebrate it?
- What is your favorite hobby?
- What do you like to do with your family?
- What languages do you speak?

IDEAS IN ACTION

Rita and Kendra are best friends. Rita is biracial. She is white and Indigenous. Kendra is Black. They eat lunch together every day.

They both really enjoy scary movies and talk about which movies they've watched recently. But they celebrate different holidays. In December, Rita celebrates Christmas. Kendra celebrates Kwanzaa. Rita tells Kendra about going to church on Christmas Eve. And Kendra tells Rita about her favorite part of Kwanzaa— lighting a candle each day with her family.

How are Rita and Kendra the same?

How are Rita and Kendra different?

What are they learning from each other?

Someone may not feel comfortable answering a question you ask. Be respectful of their choice. And let them know you understand. There are lots of other questions you can ask to get to know them.

To build an authentic connection, it's important for both people to share. So be willing to answer questions too!

Sometimes it may be hard to hear what others share with you. It may not match with your beliefs. It's good to pay attention to how you are feeling when you learn something new. Take some time to think about your feelings before you respond. Consider the other person's feelings too. If you don't, you may hurt the other person's feelings.

Figure out how you can respond respectfully. Remember the importance of making sure everyone can be their true selves. How can you accept your feelings and the other person's identities and feelings?

Once you build meaningful connections with people who are different from you, you can act in solidarity with them. Solidarity is helping others, with their permission, without asking for anything in return. Solidarity can look like:

- Stating your pronouns whenever you meet someone new.
- Asking for more books written by Black, Latine, Indigenous, and Asian people in your school's library.

As you learn new ways of connecting with others, show yourself and others compassion. Building healthy communities takes work. But it's the only way to make sure that everyone can show up as their whole, true selves.

GLOSSARY

ableism (AY-buh-liz-uhm)—unfair treatment of people with disabilities

cisgender (sis-JEHN-dur)—having a gender identity that matches the sex you were assigned when you were born

colonizer (KAH-luh-nyz-uhr)—a person who takes over and settles Indigenous people's land

heterosexual (het-uh-roh-SEK-shoo-uhl)—attracted to someone of the opposite sex or gender; this meaning is based on the idea of two genders

inclusive (in-KLOO-siv)—including everyone; not keeping out a certain group

Indigenous (in-DIJ-uh-nuss)—belonging to the group of people who first lived in a place

Latine (la-TEE-neh)—from or having ancestors from a country in Latin America, such as the Dominican Republic, Mexico, or Chile

nonbinary (non-BYE-nair-ee)—having a gender identity that is not just boy (man) or girl (woman)

oppression (oh-PRESH-uhn)—treating people in a cruel, unjust, and hard way

queer (KWEER)—holding identities such as lesbian, gay, bisexual, pansexual, or transgender; identifying as something other than heterosexual or cisgender

reservation (rez-er-VAY-shuhn)—an area of land set aside by the U.S. government for Indigenous nations

transgender (trans-JEHN-dur)—having a gender identity that does not match the sex you were assigned when you were born

READ MORE

González, Xelena. *All Around Us.* El Paso, TX: Cinco Puntos Press, 2017.

Locke, Katherine. *What Are Your Words?: A Book about Pronouns.* New York: Hachette Book Group, 2021.

Roberts, Daron K. *A Kids Book about Empathy.* Portland, OR: A Kids Book About, Inc., 2020.

INTERNET SITES

The Genderbread Person
genderbread.org

YouTube: Breathe, Feel, Share (Sesame Street in Communities)
youtube.com/watch?v=2mewUHy1LtA

YouTube: Empathy (Sesame Street in Communities)
youtube.com/watch?v=CS7Vh01zNOY

INDEX

ABOUT THE AUTHOR

Maribel Valdez Gonzalez is an Indigenous Xicana STEM/PBL coach, former classroom teacher, and consultant. She resides in occupied Duwamish territory, also known as Seattle, Washington. She is from occupied Somi Se'k land, also known as San Antonio, Texas. In her 10 years as an antiracist educator, Maribel has been honored to work with youth and adults to decolonize and humanize teaching practices and belief systems in classrooms and beyond. Maribel's goal is to create academically engaging learning experiences through a culturally sustaining environment that fosters empowerment, healing, and radical kindness. She is also a member of the Antiracist Arts Education Task Force for Visual & Performing Arts in Seattle Public Schools.